The Healing Process

by Shakiyl Muhammad

Copyright Page

© 2025 Shakiyl Muhammad

The Island Within Publishing LLC

Author's Note

I'm a man who's been through some things.

A man who drowned for a while

and had to remember how to breathe again.

These poems came from real places—

from nights where sleep felt impossible,

from days where I couldn't recognize myself,

from moments when my situation screamed louder than my own voice.

I know what it feels like to be alive, but not living.

To look in the mirror and see a stranger.

To feel your spirit somewhere far away

and not know how to call it home.

And I also know what it feels like to return to yourself.

Not all at once.

Not in a miracle moment.

But slowly—

breath by breath,

truth by truth,

step by step.

This book is about that return.

Back to your spirit.

Back to your peace.

Back to the light you thought you lost.

If something in these pages touches you, take it with you.

If something feels familiar, sit with it.

If something here makes you feel seen—hold on to that.

You deserve to feel seen.

I wrote this from honesty.

From experience.

From the part of me that stopped running.

If you're holding this book,

some part of you is ready too.

Welcome to The Healing Process—

not just the book,

but the journey back to yourself.

Dedication

I dedicate this to my children.

I dedicate this to Hope.

I dedicate this to the people walking through darkness in the middle of daylight—

to those sitting in a silent room that's louder than any crowd.

To the ones who feel unseen, unheard, untouched, but still here.

I dedicate this to isolation.

I dedicate this to the stillness.

I dedicate this to the version of me who refused to give up.

To my drive when I was empty.

To my will when breathing felt heavy.

To the part of me that kept swimming,

kept seeing a vision,

kept reaching for a light no one else could see.

Thank you to me—

the me that survived.

To my children:

Tavion, Shay'aan, Shay'mirr, Taylor, and Leo.

Even in the moments I couldn't hold you,

even when I couldn't see you,

I carried you.

I knew I had to stand as an example.

To show that no matter the storm,

no matter the pain,

no matter what life tries to take from you—

you can rise.

You can always find a way to win.

You can always find your way back to a smile.

Preface

Before we go any further, I want to say this:

Healing isn't pretty.

It's not motivational quotes or perfect timing.

It's not waking up one morning and suddenly loving yourself again.

Healing is honest.

It's uncomfortable.

It's meeting the parts of yourself you tried to hide,

and listening to the wounds you thought no one could see.

It's realizing how your experiences shaped you,

changed you,

tested you.

For a long time, I didn't know how to speak about my pain—

not without feeling weak,

not without feeling like something was wrong with me for hurting.

So I stayed quiet.

I carried everything inside.

I held weight that was never meant to be mine alone.

Maybe you know that feeling.

Maybe you learned how to be strong while breaking on the inside.

Maybe you learned how to smile without feeling joy.

Maybe you learned how to keep the world moving

while your own world was falling apart.

If so, you're not alone.

And you're seen here.

This book isn't about pretending to be okay.

It's about telling the truth—with patience, with compassion, with courage.

These words were born in the middle of the storm—

in the drowning,

the questioning,

the remembering,

the rebuilding.

This isn't a story about perfection.

It's a story about process.

About discovering that you were never broken—

you were healing in real time.

So take your time with these pages.

Read slowly.

Breathe.

Feel what you feel.

There's no rush here.

No pressure to be anywhere but where you are.

Welcome to The Healing Process.

And more than that—

welcome back to yourself.

Phase 1 Darkness

Color: Black / Deep Red

State: Drowning

Consciousness: Unaware, submerged, surviving

Structure: 3 Frequencies (I, II, III)

FREQUENCY I — I

Unaware Drowning

(Thrashing, fragmented, no language yet, just reaction)

Breath comes in pieces here.

Not steady.

Not measured.

Thoughts collide instead of forming lines.

The body knows something is wrong,

but the mind doesn't know what to call it yet.

Memory flashes.

Emotion spikes.

Nothing connects long enough to make sense.

The awareness is inside the storm,

not looking at it.

Traumatized

Traumatized

Traumatized by experience,

hypnotized by the dosage life feeds me,

blind to my own position.

I chase a peace of mind,

but never get a piece of pie—

lonely, disconnected from the peace of I,

the peace of me I cannot see.

I fall in this earthly game,

no friends, no family, nothing to lean on.

I try to reset, but upset waits for me,

two sides of a coin in my palm—

which will I pick now?

Then it hits—

I had to dig within.

I wasn't just a piece on the board,

I was the board.

I had to beat the game.

Thirty-seven years of disguise and lies,

programmed since my ABCs,

trained to follow rules that were never for me.

Manipulated style, cloned thoughts,

a circus made of clowns.

But I'm done doing tricks.

I don't need the applause.

I don't need the audience's screams.

Still Here

Stillness drowning in shame, heavy pain in my frame,

Gasping for air, every breath feel like needles in veins.

Cotton in lungs, thoughts numb, can't summon a name,

Steps in my mind but they stumble, can't run from the rain.

Bleeding emotions, red oceans, they flood through my chest,

Waves in slow motion, devotion to nothing but stress.

Heartbeat percussion, concussion of silence and press,

Time feel elastic, it stretches then snaps in my breath.

Open but trapped, wide space but it close like a cell,

Arms try to swing but they sink, like I'm froze in a spell.

Voice in my throat but it choke, it won't travel or tell,

Only echoes of panic that circle and spiral in hell.

Seconds feel heavy like years on my back when I breathe,

Minutes collapse, then they stack, then they crack at the seams.

Thoughts try to form but they storm, then they shatter in steam,

I'm in the middle of water, but water ain't what it seems.

Calling for help but the signal is lost in the noise,

Static in spirit, my body a broken-down voice.

Not falling, not floating, just stuck in the void,

Suspended in pressure, no up, no down, no choice.

Still here…

Chest tight…

Air thin…

Mind dim…

Time spin…

I'm in…

And the furthest my thought could ever arrive…

was this moment,

this space,

this breath trying to stay alive.

Version of me

(First Appearance)

In the beginning…

You smiled.

Bright.

Wild.

Free as a child.

Laughed with siblings,

Cracked jokes with folks…

Spirit too high

To be broke.

But then…

Feelings changed.

Your light got… rearranged.

Siblings, friends,

And all life's lessons

Pulled your joy

Into quiet confessions.

I told you — stay focused.

Don't get misled.

Don't let 'em play tricks

Inside your head.

Don't let 'em twist your style

Or steal your view…

But you didn't listen —

And I… lost… you.

You grew mean in your early teens,

Just to guard the peace

From your old dreams.

The people you loved

Turned laughs into cries,

Turned truth to lies

Right in your eyes.

They shoved instead of hugged,

Made fears a joke —

And then said you changed,

Like it was you they broke.

FREQUENCY II — II

Aware Drowning

(The weight is now felt, named, but not escaped)

The water has a shape now.

A pressure.

A temperature.

The chest knows it is underwater.

The heart knows it is reaching for things

that cannot pull it to the surface.

Patterns begin to show themselves,

but the body is still loyal to them.

Pain is familiar.

Attachment is heavy.

Love is learned inside survival.

The awareness can see the chains,

but the hands are still wrapped around them.

Demon Child

They called me the demon child—

laughed when they said it, but meant it meanwhile.

Every room I stepped in, silence would pile,

not 'cause I was evil—just born too wild.

Too bright, too bold, too real, too loud,

light they couldn't mold, so they dimmed it down.

Couldn't shape my shine, so they shaded my crown,

handed me their spark, told me, "This is yours now."

Turned my glow to a problem, made my soul rewind,

fed doubt to my presence, miswrote my design.

My smile was thunder, my aura a storm,

not everyone built for this frequency form.

If they couldn't handle it, blamed the vibration,

said I was the danger, labeled my nature.

So sorrow sat me down, stole rhythm and sound,

took my voice from a roar, buried deep underground.

They mimicked my movement but missed every step,

couldn't move with my spirit, so they marked me a threat.

Anger became armor, rage became friend,

walked like a wolf with no pack to defend.

"If love don't protect me, I ride on my own."

If gentleness gets mocked, then the heart turns to stone.

Wore every name thrown—like a badge, like a brand,

played the villain they painted with brushes in hand.

Brick by brick, I built walls too high to be climbed,

guarded my soul like it was serving time.

But truth behind the flame, the bite, the blame—

was a child still hurting, tired of pain.

They saw demon.

That's all they could frame.

But the truth they denied—

was a light too untamed.

They dimmed it with ego, with pride, with fear,

but what burns this bright was never meant to disappear

Hope Is Gone

Sometimes I feel like hope is gone,

feel too weak to keep holding on.

Emotions too deep to float—

I try to swim, but need a boat.

My feelings still have not gone nowhere.

Too much pride to cry,

too much of a man to shed a tear,

so I keep these emotions inside,

avoiding fear.

I often find myself

fighting with care.

Been here four years,

still have not heard from my sisters,

my brothers,

or my wife out there.

Three kids—but where?

And they question

why my hope is gone.

But I will stay strong

and keep holding on,

because I gotta see my sons—

Shay'aan, Shay'mirr, and Tavion.

Trauma Bonding

Fuck you—

no, fuck you.

We argue,

then kiss.

Hate turn heat,

pain turn bliss.

Bruises heal faster

when pleasure exists.

Bodies collide,

sheets drown in noise,

walls hear the truth

we avoid with our voice.

You say, "I love you."

I echo it back—

both of us knowing

we just filling the cracks.

We fight to stay.

We stay to fight.

Lies between moans,

hoping pain feels right.

You leave—

I call.

I block—

you stalk.

We circle the wound

till forgiveness rots.

You cry—

I try

to catch every tear,

like love is a net

that can hold all this fear.

You come home,

but home is not peace.

Not for you.

Not for me.

It's fire dressed up as laughter.

We choke on smoke

calling it happily ever after.

When we're apart, we ache.

Together, we suffocate.

Slow hurt.

Familiar pain.

Calling damage fate.

We say "love,"

but it's attachment in disguise.

Comfort hiding under shame,

truth buried under lies.

We scream love,

but fear running the show.

Needing each other

just to feel whole.

We want release,

but the grip too deep.

Calling it passion

when it's wounds we keep.

We dream of peace,

but sleep with pain.

Call it love

so nobody takes the blame.

This isn't love—

it's survival holding hands.

Fear wearing perfume,

mascara covering the damage.

Perfect bodies,

broken trust,

can't let go

because letting go scares us.

And we yelling now—

not talking.

I gotta leave you—

not 'cause I don't feel you,

but 'cause if I stay,

I will not be me anymore.

You gotta leave me—

'cause if I walk away

and you chase,

we just reopen wounds

we swore were closed before.

I gotta find me.

You gotta find you.

'Cause me being yours

keep killing my truth.

And you being mine

keep losing your shape—

we keep calling it love

while we bleed out our names.

I love you loud.

I love you wrong.

I love you broken

for way too long.

But staying means losing,

and leaving still hurts,

so we scream goodbye

like it's ripping the earth.

I gotta choose me.

You gotta choose you.

'Cause if I keep holding you,

I will never be true.

This ain't peace.

This ain't growth.

This is two souls

at the end of their rope.

This ain't love—

this is pain with a rhythm,

attachment in motion,

two hearts in collision.

This—

is trauma bonding.

FREQUENCY III — III

Surrendered Drowning

(Not giving up — going still)

The struggle slows.

Not because the water is gone,

but because the body has learned its depth.

Movement becomes observation.

Fear becomes quiet.

Questions form without being spoken.

Breath is expensive now.

Every word costs.

The fight pauses,

and in that pause,

the first real awareness is born.

Resting in the Depth

No more fight in my chest, just a weight in my breath,

Lungs heavy, every inhale feel late in its step.

Thoughts losing depth, going flat like a lake when it rests,

Emotions turn cold, like they froze and they stayed in the flesh.

Silence where panic once ran in a loop,

No alarms, just a hush in the room.

Screens blur, vision dim, time melt into fumes,

Even the urge to resist doesn't live in the room.

I'm not reaching no more, I'm not swinging to swim,

Arms tired of arguing currents that win.

Mind still here, but it's quiet within,

Like it finally accepted the night it's been in.

There's no door in my thoughts, no shore in my sight,

No picture of light, no "it'll be alright."

Just water and weight and the pull of the tide,

And a will that went still in the middle of trying.

Maybe it's dream.

Maybe it's real.

Maybe this stream is the place I was sealed.

Maybe the fight was the thing I released,

When I learned how to rest in the depth of the deep.

Not rising.

Not falling.

Just staying inside

of the space where the struggle

finally died.

Four Years of Drowning

Is this depression,

or is this my reality?

Life feels distant—

or maybe it's just moving without me.

I've been drowning in darkness,

fighting to see,

arms too heavy to swing,

too tired to breathe.

Disconnected

from the version of me I remember,

before I slipped into this ugly dream,

before the fall settled in deeper.

Someone turn on the lights—

please.

This cannot be me.

—

Four years ago.

September 10th.

A date that still echoes in my chest.

That's the day the real me slipped—

fell,

and never quite came back yet.

—

Now I'm stuck in this body—

broken, unfamiliar,

living on memories

of who I was before I disappeared here.

When people look at me,

they remember the old version.

And that reflection

makes the present one vanish.

I became my fear.

I became failure.

I became stuck—

alive, but unable to move.

Paralyzed physically.

Mentally exhausted.

Spirit pushed aside.

So tell me—

is this living?

—

Sometimes I pretend.

Borrow the energy.

Wear the personality

they still expect to see.

I gather smiles.

Collect approval.

And when the room empties—

I collapse.

I sit with the version of me I hate,

waiting on the one I miss.

Maybe this is me now.

Maybe this is the shape I'm in.

I'm drowning.

It's dark.

I'm lost.

I'm hoping to be found.

—

Alone.

No one to call.

Four years underwater,

pressure in my jaw.

I fought to swim,

arms gave out,

lungs full of doubt,

still reaching for shore I could not see now.

Maybe I wasn't meant to rise.

Maybe I wasn't meant to drown.

Maybe I had to feel the weight

before I learned how to float it down.

Not to sink forever—

just to know the depth.

To step into the water,

lose my breath,

and finally see

what lives beneath.

Closing

The body is quiet now.

Not because the pain is gone,

but because it has learned the weight of it.

Breath comes slower.

Thoughts move less.

Not calm… just spent.

There is no fight left in the arms,

no sound left in the chest,

only the awareness that the water is deep

and that I am still inside it.

Nothing is being understood yet.

Nothing is being solved.

There is only this moment

where struggle pauses

and the mind begins to wonder

what all of this means.

Phase 2 Questioning

Color: Slate Gray / Violet

State: Confusion

Consciousness: Searching, awareness forming

Structure: 3 Frequencies (I, II, III)

FREQUENCY I — I

Disorientation

(Reality feels thin. The old life no longer fits, but the new one is not yet visible.)

After the drowning came quiet.

Not peace.

Not relief.

Just space.

The body was no longer fighting the water,

but the mind had not learned how to stand on land.

Everything looked the same,

but felt… different.

Like life was still happening,

but the meaning behind it had shifted.

Routines continued.

Faces stayed familiar.

But something inside no longer believed the script.

Thoughts began to drift.

Questions formed without language.

A sense of "this isn't all of me"

echoed without explanation.

Confusion was born here—

not from chaos,

but from awareness realizing

it had been living on autopilot.

Not lost.

Not found.

Just no longer certain.

The first feeling of awakening

is not light.

It is disorientation.

The Vacation Within

I have to remove myself from him —

his story,

his experiences.

I wish I had no part in it.

His pain and fright,

can't get no sleep at night.

The disappointment, the guilt,

leave him shivering

with regret.

This can't be it.

I just wanna press reset.

Life keeps going…

but how do I remove myself from knowing?

Achievements and regrets,

love and neglects,

wins and failures —

that's normal.

That's life.

That's how it's meant to be filled.

But his?

The cries,

the tears grown dry —

could never be refilled.

His smile is lies,

his norm is pain.

Lonely, loaded with shame —

no love,

no way.

I'm planning a trip

to get away from him.

Yeah… he stuck with me

yet again.

I just really wanna smile again —

not fake,

not pretend.

The door has shut.

I lost the key.

There's no going back for me.

Confused what to do,

but forward I have to go.

Nervous as shit

to experience new change —

all my past experiences

always ended with pain.

Just release me,

please.

I wanna run away.

My smile is smothered.

My joy went another way.

Save me —

please —

give me a perspective

that might brighten my way.

My experience

is my thoughts,

is his life

that he fought.

I'll try,

with all my might,

to enjoy life,

to find my light.

I want this memory taken away.

I need joy to come my way.

Unwritten Script

Since birth, they trained us to sit in position,

hush our intuition, obey with submission.

Bottle-fed rules before sight had a vision,

mind pre-programmed, downloaded conditions.

Crawled on floors built by fear and control,

walked in directions that buried the soul.

"Don't do this, don't move, don't question, be still,"

we lost our voice tryna fit their will.

Who wrote your script?

They taught us God before teaching us self,

taught us heaven, but not inner health.

Told us when to pray, when to play, when to rest,

when to work, when to sleep, what's success, what's best.

Who wrote your script?

They said success is a house and a chain,

a title, a check, a respected name.

But what is winning if you suffocate,

living their dream while your soul suffers late?

Who wrote your script?

They built schools, jobs, prisons, laws,

rewarded obedience, punished pause.

Taught us worth is rank, love is a loan,

peace is a product, you earn it, you own.

Who wrote your script?

We said "yes" to systems, "no" to the heart,

traded imagination for a timecard start.

Forgot we were magic before their math,

before their clocks, before their paths.

Who wrote your script?

Parents, pulpits, bosses, courts,

each pen wrote lines for our thoughts and force.

But who are you when the page go blank?

Who are you when the cage get cracked?

Who wrote your script?

Every rule a chain in a suit called order,

every border drawn across your aura.

Truth ain't typed in their tradition,

it's etched in your soul, in your intuition.

So pick up the pen, feel the power shift,

this your moment, your authorship.

Don't let nobody title your chapter,

be the writer they couldn't capture.

Life ain't meant to be read like a contract.

It's meant to be lived with vision and impact.

So write your story — no edits, no drift…

"Don't ask who wrote your script.

Become the author of your script."

You Are the Residue of Yesterday's Thoughts

(First Appearance)

Had to meet me.

Not hype. Not history.

I had to meet me —

no image, no identity.

I had to meet me.

No crowd. No disguise.

Just me and the mirror

telling truth to my eyes.

Hotel room still,

machines breathing for me,

wheels under my body,

pain sitting authority.

Stitches talking loud,

silence talking more,

mirror looking dead at me like,

"Who you been this for?"

I asked one question —

simple, no excuse:

"What do you love about you?"

The answer was mute.

Days went numb.

Weeks stayed dry.

Couldn't find one reason

without asking "why."

Then I said, "You handsome."

That truth cut deep.

If looks was my love,

then love was cheap.

If beauty was value,

what happens when it fades?

If doing was purpose,

what happens when it's taken away?

I had to meet me.

Not the praise, not the win.

I had to meet me

when the claps ran thin.

I had to meet me

when the talent was gone.

Mirror said,

"Who are you now? — go on."

I loved what I did.

I loved how I was seen.

But I never loved the man

running the machine.

Mirror changed tone…

wasn't rude, wasn't loud.

Said, "You don't love yourself.

You love who they crowned."

That cracked something open.

That split something wide.

I stopped chasing approval

and went inward to hide…

FREQUENCY II — II

Mask Awareness

(Seeing the roles, the performance, the conditioning.)

The questions grow louder now.

The patterns start to show themselves.

The mind begins to recognize its habits,

its defenses,

its learned behaviors.

The soul starts to argue with the script.

The heart begins to ask

why it has been playing a role

instead of living in truth.

The chains are visible now.

Not broken—

but seen.

Bridge / Narrator / Threshold)

And once I saw the mask,

I couldn't unhear the argument behind it.

One voice promised the world.

One voice whispered truth.

Soul vs Spirit

(First Appearance)

Narrator — Intro

As I walk through the valley,

I sadly possess the attributes to misguide me.

I look up for help from God above,

but He don't come for none of us.

Maybe He already did.

Left the screwdriver, the wrench, the hammer,

the tape and the light to guide the way.

He put it all inside my soul—

His attributes, His whispers, His control.

But despite the tools that look old and bruised,

I'd rather accept what's shiny and new,

not even knowing what it do.

————

Spirit — Temptation

Sell your soul, I'm the way to go,

I'll wrap the world in gold, just say so.

I'll give you power they can't ignore,

open every gate, every door.

Crowns on your head, light on your name,

riches, attention, the glory, the fame.

I'll make every room turn your way,

every eye locked, every soul swayed.

I'll give you the love they say don't fade,

the feeling that makes strong men cave.

Why follow a whisper, quiet and small,

when I can give you everything…

all at once, all.

———

Soul — The First Whisper (Portal)

I was with you before your first breath,

before the world wrote rules on your flesh.

In the quiet of the portal,

I was the only voice.

Soft.

Still.

True.

I whispered before spirit learned your name.

Before desire dressed itself as flame.

I was the calm before the noise,

the choice before the choice.

I didn't need to pull you then—

you already knew.

But when the world rushed in,

the spirit grew louder…

and I stayed still,

waiting…

inside of you.

————

Spirit — The Reveal

I was there the moment you took your first breath,

waiting outside the portal's edge.

I dressed myself in everything you'd desire,

wrapped my hands around your ego,

fed your hunger like fire.

I am fear in silence,

I am doubt in the night.

I twist your direction,

but make the wrong road feel right.

I've worn every face you trusted,

I've whispered in every dream you chased.

You call me enemy, but truth is—

I control, I move, or replace.

I don't love you.

I control you.

I don't guide.

I bend.

I build castles from distractions,

and call them your friends.

The Performance

How did we let the phase that frees us

turn into the stage that feeds us lies?

How did we see the circus early

then volunteer to wear the disguise?

We laughed at the clown from the sidelines first,

said, "That could never be me."

Then hunger knocked, bills called loud,

and survival said, "Learn the routine."

So we studied the tricks, rehearsed the pain,

memorized moves for approval's gain,

ran through mazes they pre-designed,

calling progress what was really a chain.

See—

there is no audience clapping above.

That's the myth they sell us to soften the shove.

The ones who built this aren't watching for fun—

they're counting the output, the hours, the run.

They don't cheer.

They measure.

They don't love.

They assess.

They smile when you pass,

then reset the test.

Because the circus only works

if the performers perform.

Not belief.

Not faith.

Just energy worn.

We are not seen.

We are used.

Trained to confuse motion with choosing our route.

Left turn—reward.

Right turn—shame.

Stand still too long—starve in the rain.

So why do we worship our opposers' hands?

Why do we teach their rules as sacred plans?

Why do we trust a system that tests our worth

when it profits from distance—

from land, from birth?

Why do we eat what numbs the body?

Why do we wear what brands the mind?

Why do we drive in circles, calling it freedom,

never asking who designed the signs?

Because the trick wasn't force.

It was comfort.

Routine.

A trade:

your truth for stability,

your soul for a wage.

They didn't need loyalty.

They needed labor.

Didn't need faith.

Just behavior.

You can hate the cage and still feed it daily.

You can see the lie and still move like it saved you.

Awareness alone doesn't break the spell—

withdrawal does.

And that's the part they never tell.

Because stopping the performance

isn't loud.

It's quiet.

No cheers.

No boos.

Just the absence of compliance.

It's the moment you ask,

"If I don't move—who am I?"

When the role dissolves

and the mask won't reply.

That silence scares more than pain ever could.

Because pain still fits inside what you understood.

Stillness demands choice.

Choice demands truth.

Truth demands you stop running from you.

So no—

the circus doesn't fall when the crowd goes mute.

It falls when the performers refuse to salute.

When they walk off stage

without rage, without fight,

just reclaiming their breath,

their direction, their light.

That's why they fear the eagle remembering the sky.

That's why they fracture the self into reasons why.

That's why they split you into versions at war—

because a whole one won't perform anymore.

And this—

this—

is the moment in the book

where the reader is no longer watching.

They're deciding.

Do I keep dancing for permission to eat?

Or do I build a life

that doesn't need their seat?

Because the exit was never hidden.

It was stillness.

And the key was always yours—

the day you stopped performing

and remembered who you were.

Spiritually

When I hear "spiritually" —

I think of things I can't see,

but everybody swear they know exactly what it means.

Not religion.

Not the rules they tried to hand me.

But then again…

who told me that?

They said spirit been in me

since the womb,

but they also said I was born wrong,

born sinful,

born needing permission to be clean.

So which one is it?

They say "listen to God,"

but every voice claiming Him

sound different.

Every book got a rule,

every rule got a threat,

every threat got a heaven

I might not even qualify for yet.

We confuse it with vision.

We confuse it with noise.

We confuse fear for warning,

and conditioning for a divine voice.

Is this intuition…

or is this just what they planted in my head

when I was too young to choose?

They say spirit is light.

They say spirit is love.

But why everything spiritual come with a warning,

a punishment,

a fire above?

They say believe.

But believe who?

The preacher?

The book?

The ancestor?

The system that taught me to bow before I learned to stand?

They say angels watch.

They say demons roam.

They say heaven up.

They say hell below.

But nobody can show me the map,

and everybody swear they know the road.

So spiritually,

I'm torn.

Not lost —

just unconvinced.

Trying to hear something real

through layers of tradition, fear, and influence.

If God is in me,

why they keep pointing outside?

If truth is in me,

why they keep telling me to doubt my inside?

They say "good."

They say "bad."

They label, divide,

and call it holy.

But all I feel is confusion

wearing sacred clothing.

So spiritually,

I'm not at peace.

I'm in question.

I'm in tension.

I'm in that space

between what I was taught

and what I feel

but don't know how to explain yet.

I'm not saying I know the way.

I'm saying I'm tired of being told

the way

by people who never had to walk my mind.

Wake Up

Pay attention — stay woke,

desires you wish for been trained to be yours,

but what they gave you was a cage in gold form.

Wake up.

The time they gave you — that's the program,

clock hands keep you in slow jams,

seconds, minutes, hours — it's all scam,

to keep your purpose on hold, man.

Wake up.

The change they give ain't change, it's control,

coins that jingle just to chain your soul.

They hand you silver to make you feel gold,

but that pocket weight keep your spirit old.

Wake up.

The bracelet — that's a shackle,

the ring — that's the matrix,

you trapped in the sparkle,

calling it sacred.

Wake up.

They taught us to chase the whip,

but that whip the same one that split our skin.

Now it's leather, now it's luxury,

same tool — just a cleaner sin.

Wake up.

They directing your route, guiding your path,

you just a puppet reacting to cash.

They mapped out your moves, sold you your past,

called it success, but it's all just glass.

Wake up.

We chasing the leash that's choking our breath,

dying alive while avoiding death.

The program got you thinking it's best

to follow the script that keeps you depressed.

Wake up.

They paint the illusion, call it design,

you running in circles, thinking you fine.

Time, change, ring, and chain combined

got your freedom locked in a shrine.

Wake up.

You are not your desires —

they wrote those in fire.

They built your heaven to look like a buyer,

but that's the real hell you admire.

Wake up.

You can't free your soul

if you still love your cage.

You can't rise in truth

if you worship the stage.

Wake up.

Break that bracelet, toss that ring,

watch how your spirit start to sing.

Lose the whip, forget the bling,

reclaim your time — that's the real king.

Wake up

The Eagle

(First Appearance)

Sitting on the highest mountain…

This—this can't be where I stay.

My wings and beak? They okay.

So why don't I have the courage…

or the energy… to fly away?

I've grown—

Paralyzing this place.

Defeat… that's what I see in me.

But the bold eagle in me—

the fight—

it won't let me give up on flight.

"Fly high, no one can stop me."

That's what I tell myself.

"I'm not weak," I repeat…

but healing keeps avoiding me.

Or maybe… I'm doing the avoiding.

Then I sat with myself.

Noticed my dull beak—

and realized…

there's more broken than it seemed.

Anger and disbelief.

Yelling.

Beating my beak violently.

"I'm too tough. I can't be beat."

But then… a feather fell

from my strong wings.

Just one.

"What's one feather gonna do to me?"

That was my mindset.

But then more feathers fell—

and more.

"What the fuck are these feathers falling for?"

My strong wings… they won't fly.

My beak is dull.

What am I supposed to do?

Too much pride to cry,

so I hide them—

my problems—

pushed aside.

In anger and fright,

my boldness held

a poison that was only mine.

———

I'm on this mountain, out of sight.

My beak is dull.

I cannot fight.

My wings are weak.

I can't take flight.

This can't be my end.

I gotta try.

FREQUENCY III — III

Existential Questioning

(Not asleep anymore. Not awake yet. The mind begins to ask who it is.)

The noise settles.

The world continues.

But something inside has shifted.

Identity feels unstable.

Belief feels uncertain.

The past no longer explains the present.

There are no answers yet.

Only the awareness

that a question has been born.

And once a question is born,

nothing can return to how it was.

If Losing Is A Choice

Why Lose?

If losing is a choice,

then why lose?

I had times I was up,

times I carried big smiles,

pockets full, money long,

surrounded by love, big crowds.

I hit the last shot,

dropped an opponent with a hook,

caught the pass in the clutch,

crossed the line —

their fans had to clap.

But this is not a game.

Life, no game.

No scoreboard,

no ref to call a foul,

no coach in my ear giving advice.

You fall —

either get up

or stay down,

and miss life.

A thought is just a thought

until you feed it.

An emotion is just a feeling

unless you let it sit —

then it shapes you,

moves you,

becomes the room you live in.

So again I ask:

If losing is a choice,

then why lose?

Maybe we lose

’cause we never knew winning.

Maybe we lose

’cause pain felt like living.

Maybe we lose

’cause hurt felt like home,

while peace felt strange,

like a place we don’t belong.

Or maybe we lose

’cause we thought losing was love —

holding on to storms

instead of reaching above.

I don’t know.

I don't know…

I just know

there has to be something else

besides repeating what hurts.

There has to be another way

besides calling suffering normal.

If losing is a choice…

I'm still trying to understand

what winning even means.

Closing

The mind is no longer asleep.

But it is not yet awake.

The storm has quieted,

not because it is gone,

but because the body has learned how to listen inside it.

Questions now live where fear used to sit.

Doubt replaces certainty.

The script begins to loosen its grip.

The mirror has spoken.

The patterns have shown themselves.

The masks have been noticed.

The height has been tasted,

even if the wings are not ready yet.

Nothing is clear.

Nothing is solved.

But something irreversible has happened:

The voice inside has started asking why.

And once a question is born,

the old life can no longer pretend to be the only life.

This is not peace.

This is not freedom.

This is the moment before remembering.

The water is still deep,

but now the eyes are open.

And in that opening,

the first light begins to form.

THRESHOLD — WITNESS

At the edge of the turn,

two feelings stood in the same body—

one afraid of closeness,

one certain of the light ahead.

Nothing was judged.

Nothing was rushed.

Both were allowed to speak.

Scary Affection

What is this?

Kisses and hugs—

why my chest get tight when you showing me love?

Unnecessary touch,

why my body tense up?

Why I'd rather just fuck

than let my heart open up?

You say, "I love you."

My mind freezes when you say that.

Why you looking that deep?

Why your eyes stay attached?

That energy loud,

but it don't make a sound.

Feels warm when you close,

feel heavy when you around.

I'm here—

you ain't gotta pretend no more.

But all that affection

feel like pressure in my mind.

Extra attention,

why it make me retreat?

Why my stomach flip fast

when you reaching for me?

Guard jump up.

Heart go brittle.

I don't know how to stay when it's gentle.

You touch my chest,

I flinch, I stall—

I want it,

but I don't know how to hold it at all.

This love feel strange.

This softness feel loud.

Why I feel exposed

when you calm me down?

I find something to do.

I leave early, I go.

Not 'cause of you—

this feeling don't listen to control.

I don't wanna be soft.

I don't wanna be sweet.

Holding hands, rubbing feet—

this don't feel like me.

I can handle pain.

Pain speak clear.

But this right here

feel unfamiliar.

Complicated.

Quietly deep.

I want the love,

but it hurt to receive.

Used to chaos,

used to the fight.

Peace feel awkward

when you lived your life tight.

So I learned how to love through actions and deeds—

protection, presence,

showing up when I need.

But when affection come close—

too steady, too near—

I disappear fast,

no warning, no gear.

Scary affection.

Why it make me defensive?

Why love feel dangerous

when nobody offensive?

I crave connection,

but my body don't trust it.

Heart want to stay,

mind saying, "Run from it."

Still I try.

Still I breathe.

Learning how to stay

when my soul wanna leave.

I can love—

that part I know.

But learning to be loved

move slower in my soul.

Maybe one day

I won't flinch when you're close.

I'll let love hold me

without feeling exposed.

Inner Conversation (Driver & Passenger)

Mind got the wheel,

hands tight on the lane,

reading every sign,

measuring risk, counting the rain.

Heart in the passenger seat,

quiet but clear,

looking past the fog,

saying, "I know where we're going from here."

Mind say,

"What if the road split?

What if the map wrong?

What if we run out of time,

what if the night too long?"

Heart say,

"I feel the direction.

I don't need every sign.

I don't need every answer.

I just know this is mine."

Mind say,

"What if love slow us down?

What if it cost us the race?"

Heart say,

"Some destinations only reached

when you stop rushing the pace."

Mind say,

"What if our routes don't match,

what if the lanes divide?"

Heart say,

"Different roads can still lead

to the same sunrise."

Mind calculating curves,

counting exits, planning the turns,

carrying fear like extra weight,

braking before the lesson is learned.

Heart steady,

feeling the pull of the light ahead,

not arguing with doubt,

just knowing where we're led.

Mind:

"What if we take separate streets,

separate timing, separate views?"

Heart:

"Timing can differ,

but truth don't choose two truths."

Mind:

"What if logic says let go?"

Heart:

"What if intuition says hold?"

Mind sees distance.

Heart sees the destination already told.

Then silence in the car,

engine hum, night wide,

mind still gripping the steering wheel,

heart watching the horizon rise.

And the truth land soft but strong:

You might drive with fear.

You might drive with plans.

You might question every mile

with your logical hands.

But I see the end of the road.

I see the light where we arrive.

Different thoughts, same direction.

Different roles, same drive.

So drive how you need to drive.

Ask every "what if" you want to ask.

I'm not here to fight the wheel—

I'm here to remind you of the path.

Because even if the roads look different,

and the signs confuse the mind,

the destination is one place,

and love already knows the sign.

Same horizon.

Same light.

Same end in sight.

PHASE 3 — AWARENESS

Color: Bronze / Burnished Gold

State: Awakening

Consciousness: Recognition, Alignment, Becoming

Structure: 3 Frequencies (I, II, III)

The water is still here,

but the eyes are open now.

Not floating.

Not sinking.

Beginning to see.

FREQUENCY I — I

Self-Recognition

(Seeing the self without illusion, without mask, without escape)

This is the first clear look.

No performance.

No running.

No story to hide behind.

Just the self meeting the self.

Mirror

Anger teach hate,

humility birth humbleness,

fear welcome survival,

isolation open memory chambers

we wasn't ready to enter yet.

Frustration rising in the chest,

shame falling through levels,

why this darkness keep swinging on us

like it studied the schedule?

We stopped hiding behind walls

that never guarded our skin,

disappointment showed up early,

discouragement rented space in the head again.

Solitude creeping slow,

avoidance teaching insight,

lessons we never requested

kept replaying at night.

'Cause the real us deep inside

wanted love, wanted care,

but pain trained the instincts

to believe hiding was safer than there.

Alone, we met us —

no audience, no noise,

trying to live through trauma

with a fractured, chaotic voice.

Still goal-driven,

even when support went missing

from the ones we once believed

was part of the vision.

Achievement after achievement,

confidence started to click,

we saw value in ourselves

through the things we built brick by brick.

Not applause.

Not permission.

Just effort turning belief.

Discipline forming integrity

that refused to let us leave.

Dignity took its first breath,

felt the backbone expand,

character grew legs

every time we chose to stand.

The heart learned distance

without freezing the flame,

creativity sharpened edges

pain couldn't tame.

The smile found light again,

standards planted their feet,

this what survived the pressure —

the part of us

that wouldn't retreat.

No lesson.

No sermon.

No need to explain.

Just proof of what remains

when survival burn off

and truth stay trained.

Behind the cloud (vent room)

We gon' vent—

every vent turn hallways to chambers,

every echo get louder,

truth bouncing off anger and danger.

Sound traveling, circling, breaking the silence,

heartbeat in cadence,

this frequency forming a language.

We the Sun behind clouds,

they only prepare for the rain,

can't read the light in the sky

till it cut through the gray.

They call the glow "too much,"

call the warmth "too bright,"

but they cold in their vision

so they nervous of light.

Our energy, frequency, thoughts in a beam,

moving through doubt like a river through seams,

cutting the dark with a luminous swing,

reminding the shadow what brilliance means.

They trapped in confusion,

illusions they build,

believing conclusions

their trauma distilled.

Fake truths, real lies,

old cycles in disguise,

where the past keep murdering now

and tomorrow barely survives.

So how do you rewire a mind

trained to fear its own flame?

How you teach the Sun it was never the storm,

never the cloud, never the rain?

Should we fold for acceptance,

reshape our reflection,

dim our projection

to match their perception?

Nah.

This our light, this our life, this our direction.

We choose the version of us

that rise in correction.

Light gon' shine

even boxed in shade,

Sun still breathe

even close to the grave.

Power in the chest,

truth in the name,

don't let their limits

sketch your frame.

Let your aura spiral,

let it glow and extend,

confidence bending the clock,

making minutes suspend.

Spirit expanding,

transmitting the wave,

sending beams through the love

and the ones who behave.

Even if they forget us,

even if they oppose,

that spark, that connection,

that current still flows.

Frequency linking what distance can't close,

once light touch light,

it eternally knows.

We the Sun behind clouds,

still warming the day,

still humming through silence,

still coloring gray.

You are the Sun—

not the weather, not the night,

not the doubt, not the storm,

not the absence of sight.

You the source.

You the fire.

You the glow in the dark.

Even when covered,

you still who you are.

Versions Of Me

(*Second Appearance*)

——

I listened… to the image.

Thought it was truth.

It told me cold

Was the armor of youth.

Said:

Never let pain

Get close to your skin.

Said:

Losing is fine —

As long as you win.

That image led me into a cell:

Four walls.

No sky.

My own little hell.

Family faded.

Friends went ghost.

The same ones who swore

They loved me the most.

Then came the day

My body gave in…

Paralyzed —

And that's when it began again.

Everybody gone.

Not a soul in sight.

All that loyalty

Vanished overnight.

I lost my daughter.

My blood. My heart.

A piece of my soul —

Torn clean apart.

That loss hit harder

Than chains or steel…

Because that's the one wound

Time couldn't heal.

Friends… family… all slipped away —

Till only my shadow

Was left to stay.

And I stared at the mirror,

Dead in my stare,

Wondering who that was

Standing there.

FREQUENCY II — II

Inner Architecture

(Rebuilding, separating survival from soul, learning structure)

Now awareness moves from seeing

to understanding how the inner world was built.

What was learned.

What was inherited.

What was never truly chosen.

THE BUILDING OF ME

I learned to cross the street

inside myself—

started in the middle of the building

I kept losing in.

Ran down the stairs

chasing defeat,

climbed back up

with regret on my feet.

Fear whispered loud,

sleep pulled me deep,

walking half-alive

in a world half-asleep.

Tired of floors

I kept waking up on,

so I broke through ceilings

to see what was wrong.

Empty rooms,

quiet halls,

every window sealed shut.

No exits at all.

I was stuck in a building

with nowhere to go—

faith on empty,

frequency low.

Insecurities rising,

doubts through the roof—

"How do I let go?"

I needed the proof.

I promised I'd grow…

I just didn't know how to move.

———

Then vision got clearer,

hope found a spark.

Heard the last cries

of the soul in the dark.

Spirit stepped in,

changed my direction:

"Enjoy the misery—

it's building your lessons."

Pain took notes,

wisdom felt small,

so I hid my truth

behind thick walls.

Trying to squeeze into rooms

never built for me,

trying to be someone

I couldn't be.

———

Ran up flights

with everything in me,

tired of the losses,

tired of repeat.

Same rooms, same echoes—

I needed the break.

Saw an exit through fog

I fought myself to take.

No longer asleep,

energy weak,

but willpower heavy

when my future felt bleak.

Swinging and falling,

but still rising up—

till I finally found

my exit from us.

———

Moved through the doors,

but something grabbed tight.

"Release me," I whispered,

"Don't hold my life."

Turned around—

no hand in sight,

just fear and doubt

clinging to my spine.

It was me holding me

the whole damn time—

till truth cracked open

the locks in my mind.

———

I broke the old me

like a chain set free,

stepped off the building

with a strange release.

Fresh air hit,

but the breeze felt scary—

freedom ain't soft

when the wounds still carry.

People outside

scattered with fear,

looking for exits

that weren't even near.

I held on a pole

like life needed control—

till something unseen

guided my soul

to another building

across the road.

———

But that door was locked.

How do I get in?

I want to climb,

I want to win.

Blocks and chains,

guards and keys—

every one of them

a version of me.

Confidence came

when I spoke to my soul,

truth loosened chains

that fought for control.

Working on me,

learning to speak,

learning to walk

without dragging the weak.

Still torn between

the man I was before

and the empty building

I couldn't return to anymore.

————

Thought the noise,

the crowd,

the ones who loved the old me loud,

would someday release me—

let me out.

Saw the guards walk off…

but the door stayed shut.

Threw a brick at the window,

hope in my gut—

brick broke first,

and the guards showed up.

Stuck again,

but breath came slow.

I started to hear

what my enemy knows.

Listening turned behavior,

behavior turned keys—

and the locked doors opened

the moment I believed.

Took my first step

toward the unknown floor,

walked through a doorway

I'd never seen before.

———

Now I'm in another building—

this one free.

Vision sharp,

future loud,

soul speaking to me.

And I'll move on every idea,

every dream,

every leap—

as long as my spirit

continues to speak.

Underground Wisdom

Seeds in the soil, hands in the dirt,

sun in they face, they rehearsed for the burst.

Watered with praise, measured in worth,

taught how to rise, taught how to search.

Straight-line growth, rows and design,

planned by the clock, trained by the time.

Leaves get love, petals get shown,

cameras flash when the colors get grown.

That's spirit form — structure and frame,

faith with a ladder, light with a name.

But mushrooms move on a different code,

no seed, no stage, no audience, no road.

Built in the dark where the silence live,

learning from rot what the light can't give.

Webs in the dirt, thoughts underground,

cities of life where no sound is found.

They don't beg sun, they don't chase skies,

they read the moisture, they feel when to rise.

No permission slips, no spotlight cues,

just pressure, patience, and quiet truths.

From broken wood and forgotten places,

they learn how to heal what decay embraces.

Same thing can save you, same thing can kill,

dose is the difference between cure and ill.

Ignored, they poison.

Respected, they mend.

Misread, they end you.

Understood, they ascend.

Spirit grow upward, chasing the glow,

built by belief and the rules we're told.

Soul grow inward, spreading in shade,

fed by the wounds we never displayed.

One loves applause, one loves the dark,

one needs a teacher, one learns from the scar.

One seeks heaven, one maps the ground,

one speaks in words, one hums in sound.

Flowers perform for the eyes and the crowd,

mushrooms perform where it's quiet and loud

inside your chest, where the shadows stay,

where truth get born with no light of day.

So don't overlook what the soil concealed,

don't call it strange just 'cause it don't appeal.

What grows in silence, what lives in the low,

often holds medicine the sun don't know.

Quiet don't mean weak.

Dark don't mean wrong.

Some of the deepest power

never learned to sing loud songs.

Narrator — Recognition

I recognize the part of me that shines.

I also recognize the part of me that was built where no one was watching.

They are not opposites.

They are one story.

The Love of the Old Self

How do you save a love

that don't even love itself,

when you drowning for air

trying not to lose yourself?

Underwater in darkness,

no light where the truth is,

both of us feel like we belong here—

but something in me say, "Move quick."

Chest tight, breath thin,

lungs burning, I'm sinking in,

one hand reaching for the surface,

the other still gripping the stone of "then."

How do I swim

when attachment got weight?

How do I rise

when memories anchor my fate?

The one I'm tied to won't relax,

won't float, won't flow, won't heal,

one hand holding the future,

one hand holding what's unreal.

Trying to pull us both to air,

but gravity got a stronger grip,

love feel warm in the moment,

but it cold when you start to slip.

The attention, the smile, the way they need me—

that's the chain I couldn't see,

I thought I was holding love,

but love was holding me.

I need air.

I need space.

I need peace in a different place.

Is it the situation that need release,

or is it me that need to break free?

Thoughts keep circling,

memories won't drown,

every time I try to rise,

the past try to pull me down.

So I let go.

I kick, I float, I fight the tide,

hoping the weight of yesterday

don't follow me to the other side.

But it whisper, "Stay."

"It's safe right here."

"This depth is home."

"This pain is familiar, don't disappear."

"It'll change."

"We'll grow."

"Just wait, you'll see."

But growth don't happen

where fear keeps the key.

So I stayed.

Played the role.

Held the breath.

Waited too long

and almost chose death.

Not the body—

the spirit kind.

The slow suffocation of losing my mind.

Now I know:

love for who they were

can't grow where they refuse to be.

So I shift my reality,

cut the cord, set my soul free,

become the version of me

I was always meant to see.

I had to move.

Soul vs Spirit

(Second Appearance)

Spirit — The Reveal

I was there the moment you took your first breath,

waiting outside the portal's edge.

I dressed myself in everything you'd desire,

wrapped my hands around your ego,

fed your hunger like fire.

I am fear in silence,

I am doubt in the night.

I twist your direction,

but make the wrong road feel right.

I've worn every face you trusted,

I've whispered in every dream you chased.

You call me enemy, but truth is—

I control, I move, or replace.

I don't love you.

I control you.

I don't guide.

I bend.

I build castles from distractions,

and call them your friends.

Narrator — Awareness (The Game Shifts)

Oh… I fucking see you now.

All that shine, all that whisper —

just a hand moving pieces

on a board that's mine.

I'm not your pawn,

I am the board.

I am the watcher,

the player,

the one keeping score.

You painted detours in gold,

wrapped cages in crowns,

sold me noise dressed as sound.

You moved me like you owned me,

but I was the game the whole time.

You never held the power —

you just borrowed my mind.

I know the difference now…

your scream ain't my voice.

The soul was always the compass —

you was just the choice.

The spirit is decorated to distract…

and my soul is my GPS to direct.

FREQUENCY III — III

The Day My Vision Changed

(Expansion of sight, alignment of will, awareness turning into direction)

This is the moment the question becomes movement.

Not just seeing who I am.

Not just understanding how I was built.

But realizing I am bigger than the room I learned to survive in.

This is where the inner world widens.

Perspective lifts.

Thought becomes choice.

Awareness becomes trajectory.

WHO AM I?

Who am I?

I'm a massive energy

wrapped in flesh and bone,

consciousness breathing

through a human form.

Awareness alive.

I'm present. I'm here.

I got thoughts, I got feelings,

but I am not fear.

I feel them.

I hear them.

I watch them collide—

but I'm the one standing

behind my own mind.

So who am I?

———

Am I big or tall?

Black or brown?

Built with muscle

or heavy and round?

Am I handsome?

Am I flawed?

Am I blessed

or cursed by God?

I ask myself questions,

look outward for proof,

hoping somebody see something

that point me to truth.

But who am I… really?

————

Am I the man who'll sell for cash?

React to pressure, violent and rash?

The one who walk in a crowded space

and silence fall when I show my face?

Maybe that's me.

Or maybe it's not.

So let's not ignore

the part they forgot.

————

Am I the smile

when the room feel down?

The voice of hope

when nobody else around?

Am I the ear

when you need to vent?

The man who give his last

even when it's rent?

The one who step forward

when danger appear,

stand in the way

when you frozen in fear?

Who am I?

————

Can I be good and bad?

Strong and sad?

In shape and tired,

confident and mad?

Handsome and ugly?

Broken and whole?

A heart full of love

with a guarded soul?

Who am I?

————

Am I emotionally wrecked,

unbalanced inside?

Fake love show up—

I attach, then I hide.

I think I love back,

but it's fear in disguise.

I never learned love—

I just learned how to survive.

When emotions rush in,

I retreat, I evade,

fall back fast

from the feelings I crave.

Can I be soft

and still stay alive?

Who am I?

———

Am I the dark voice

creeping at night?

The one that say,

"You not worth the fight."

"Give it up."

"Life hard."

"What you swinging for?"

Or—

———

Am I the voice

that answer back?

The one that say,

"Stand your ground. Don't crack."

"Get up."

"Hold tight."

"Lift your head high."

"Shakiyl, you built for storms—

you don't fold, you survive."

"Keep swinging.

This fight not done.

You been strong

since day one."

So who am I?

———

Then it clicked.

I'm a giant frequency

in an imperfect frame,

abilities layered

in pleasure and pain.

Thoughts spark emotion.

Emotion give fuel.

The body reacts

to the patterns I choose.

But I—

I am the awareness

watching it all.

———

I'm not my past.

I'm not my mistakes.

I'm not today's mood

or yesterday's ache.

I'm the thought and the thinker,

the fall and the climb,

the shadow and light

moving through time.

I'm the good and the bad,

the flawed and the gifted.

And now that I see it,

my power shifted.

Whatever I feed,

whatever I entertain—

that's the version of me

that move in my name.

———

So today,

I choose me—

the clearest form,

standing in truth

no matter the storm.

I am the illustrator of my image,

the author of my story,

the director of my movie,

framing my life in its full-time glory.

I design the scenes,

I decide the tone,

I choose the path

this character grown.

So ask yourself—

Who am I?

Because now…

I know me.

Peace.

The Vision We See

I used to think survival was the goal—

just breathe, just move, just make it home.

Fight shadows I couldn't control,

thinking pain was the price of a strong soul.

But now I know…

it's not about survival.

It's about arrival.

About becoming the version of me

that pain tried to keep in denial.

When I was young,

I built armor out of anger

and called it strength.

Told myself I'd never cry again,

thinking that made me brave—

not knowing it only made me tense.

My soul kept whispering,

"You don't have to be unbreakable…

you just have to be real."

I used to feed my mind fear,

and it showed up everywhere near.

Now I feed it vision,

and peace appear—

clear as the mirror

I once avoided.

Do we all do that?

Build walls so high

we forget there's a view behind them.

But life isn't the wall—

it's the window.

It's seeing yourself clearly

and finally letting yourself in.

Because the real poem

was never the pain we became…

it was the vision we see.

That moment we stop running from the mirror

and start standing with it.

Not fixing.

Not hiding.

Just recognizing.

I'm not here to be perfect.

I'm here to be present.

To breathe again.

To believe again.

To feel space where fear once lived.

The vision we see—

that's where the shift begins.

Not freedom yet.

Not the finish.

Just the first clear sight

of who we are becoming.

TikTok, (Time Begin)

vision in my head but I question where to step in,

I write it down, draft plans, try to lock the pen in,

then my flaws tap shoulders like, "Remember when?"

Fear start whispering, distractions pull me back,

insecurities reaching, pushing progress off track,

new me at the door but the past gripping the latch,

momentum feel fragile, confidence cracked.

TikTok, time is now,

trying to move different but I do not know how,

forcing myself forward, foot half out the house,

wind hit my chest, blew me right back on the couch.

Clock keep ticking, friction in my brain,

mind want elevation, body love the same,

patterns on repeat, habits in a frame,

change knocking loudly but comfort call my name.

TikTok, third quarter, pressure in the lane,

courage finally rising, confidence regain,

wisdom speaking clearly, spirit feeling sane,

soul locked in alignment, focus in my vein.

Then a bang, then a knock,

old faces at the door trying to rewind the clock,

people I once knew still holding the lock,

if I open that door, I return to that box.

TikTok, TikTok, heartbeat sync with the sound,

time bending forward while the past pull me down,

clock hands spinning, seconds falling around,

this is where decisions get heavy with pounds.

Who are you willing to be when the mask got to go?

What are you willing to leave when the truth say no?

Is it friends you been holding or fears you been fed?

Is it comfort and stories that keep looping your head?

Is it scars from experiences soaked in regret?

Is it tears from the years you not finished with yet?

Tik-tick, moment sharp like a blade,

give up the cycle or stay feeling played.

So I broke the perspective, shattered the frame,

did not quit on myself, I just quit on the pain,

soul stayed steady, spirit patient in place,

mind and emotions finally running the same race.

TikTok, new day forming, vision clear in my sight,

time not chasing me now — I am chasing my life.

I'm not evolving for war, I'm evolving from it!

From the storms I survived and the masks I was stuck in,

From the people, the places, the roles I was loving,

From killing my feelings just to feel like I wasn't.

They was dry in the tent while I drowned in the rain,

Judging my wounds like they earned my pain,

Calling me proud when I stood in my flame,

Hoping I'd fall just to level the game.

The war was the rooms where I shrank to belong,

The versions of me that knew something was wrong,

The nights I went numb just to keep moving on,

The times I betrayed myself just to feel strong.

They want me to dance to the song that they chose,

They set the tempo, then tighten control,

Count every step, try to script every pose,

Determined to move me, to own how I go.

If I shine off-beat, they get nervous and close,

Checking my rhythm like it came with a code,

Praying for gravity, hoping I fold,

Uncomfortable watching me find my own road.

They spoke love with their mouths, but their eyes told a truth,

Wishing my downfall, uncomfortable with my proof,

Even my blood said I earned what I went through,

Asked me to die while I fought just to move.

I'm not your assumption, your label, your frame,

Not your projection, your comfort, your pain,

I am not built from the versions I became

When I was auditioning just to earn my name.

I'm walking away from the war in my head,

From the crowd, from the noise, from the versions now dead,

From the boy who felt love was what he had to beg,

To the man who stands whole even lonely instead.

This evolution is quiet, no audience, no claps,

Just truth in my chest and my soul on the map,

No need to perform, no need to collapse,

I'm not lonely in loss — I'm lonely in fact.

In fact, I'm at peace with the space that I'm in,

The silence is clean, it's where healing begins,

I'm not rising to battle, I'm shedding my skin,

I'm not evolving for war... I'm evolving from it.

The Eagle

(Second Appearance)

I'm on this mountain, out of sight.

My beak is dull.

I cannot fight.

My wings are weak.

I can't take flight.

This can't be my end.

I gotta try.

So I beat my beak—

in pain…

in fright.

I smashed again…

and again…

until the final strike.

Screamed loud cries,

but no one in sight.

Still—

I knew my beak would grow…

and head.

———

My beak is back!

I shout with all my might—

Anger. Rage.

And ready for the fight.

But then I tried to fly…

and learned there's more.

I had another wound

I couldn't ignore.

With my strong beak,

I plucked the feathers

from my wings.

Ouch.

I screamed in pain.

This healing hurts.

How do I regain

my strength…

so I can soar again?

———

My feathers grew back.

My wings got strong.

But the pain stayed—

like thunder,

hiding behind calm.

Then I saw her.

Another eagle…

just like me.

She told me to fly away,

but I held on—

to someone I was supposed to release.

She waited.

She prayed.

But I wasn't ready.

The storm came.

I couldn't hide the rain.

Lightning struck.

Thunder roared.

And I gave her my pain.

She just wanted to guide me,

but I made her stay.

In the beginning,

she told me:

"This road is lonely.

You gotta find your way."

But I held on.

Thought she was mine.

I was wrong.

She was my blueprint.

My guide.

You Are Residue Of Yesterday's Thoughts

(Second Appearance)

Character audits.

Habit eviction.

Rewriting survival

into self-discipline.

Four years in the fire.

Emotion in pain.

Mind lifting trauma

like it's part of the gains.

Spirit yelling, "Move!"

Soul whispering, "Breathe."

Some days I stood tall.

Some days I barely believed.

I numbed it.

I ran it.

I tried to erase.

Tried to murder old versions

I still saw in my face.

Shame ran laps.

Guilt made the bed.

But every time I stood up,

this stayed in my head:

Get up.

You owe you.

Not the world.

Not the past.

Get up —

you owe you.

And hear this-

this the part you seem to miss:

You don't live in today.

You live in the residue.

Your habits, your fears,

your moves — that's yesterday talking to you.

Your life right now

is old thoughts on replay.

Today is just the echo

of what you believed yesterday.

Closing

The water is still here.

But it does not feel the same.

The mirror spoke.

The light answered.

The clock started talking back.

And something inside stopped waiting.

I can feel the shift—

not as peace,

but as direction.

Old versions still reach for me,

but they do not feel like home.

The question is not gone.

It just has a new shape now.

My eyes are open.

My chest is up.

And even if I'm still in the water—

I'm not asleep in it anymore.

THRESHOLD — WITNESS

I could see now.

But seeing didn't mean safe—

it meant I couldn't lie to myself anymore.

THE TRIAL OF TOUGHNESS

LAWYER:

Court in session, soul on trial, truth in the air,

I call the version of me that move like life ain't fair.

Define "tough" for the record, no posture, no bluff—

what is strength when the world get rough?

DEFENDANT:

Tough is defense, it's pressure and pride,

never get played, never let nothin' slide.

It's answering looks with a cold-blooded stare,

it's making a room feel danger in the air.

LAWYER:

Defense from what? From a word? From a tone?

From a look that remind you you're still alone?

DEFENDANT:

From disrespect. From feeling small.

From ever letting fear make the call.

LAWYER:

So how you respond when the mouth get brave?

DEFENDANT:

I respond with the body, send it to the grave.

LAWYER:

Who that hurt when the breath run out?

DEFENDANT:

His name, his bloodline, his mama's shout.

Kids grow up with a picture and pain,

one moment of rage turn generations insane.

LAWYER:

So a sentence decide a permanent fate?

DEFENDANT:

I let a bullet translate what the tongue couldn't say.

LAWYER:

And what that build in you?

DEFENDANT:

Confidence. Courage.

Kill the weak part too.

LAWYER:

So weakness live in you then?

DEFENDANT (tight):

Watch your tone.

LAWYER:

Oh… truth touched a nerve.

Noted. Let's continue.

What does hurt feel like when it tap your chest?

How you answer pain when it show unannounced?

DEFENDANT:

I don't feel hurt, I deliver it clean,

leave scars so deep they live in the scene.

Disrespect get branded, never erased,

so nobody forget what it cost to test my space.

LAWYER:

Is that power or fear in a heavier frame?

Is it strength or trauma wearing a different name?

DEFENDANT:

Ain't no weakness in me, I prove with steel.

LAWYER:

Is toughness your walk, your stare, your speech?

DEFENDANT:

It's action.

My voice say, "Don't reach."

LAWYER:

Who were you before the storms and the scars?

At five years old, were you built this hard?

DEFENDANT:

Why you digging in my mind like this?

LAWYER:

Because the truth don't knock — it kicks.

————

LAWYER:

They say being tough mean nobody play you,

nobody cross you, nobody stay you.

Sounds like a throne with nobody near.

Are you too tough for joy? Too armored for tears?

DEFENDANT:

Joy is distance. Walls, not doors.

Never close enough to feel no more.

LAWYER:

That ain't peace, that's isolation dressed.

Fear wearing a crown calling itself "respect."

Rooms go quiet when you walk in, true,

but silence ain't love — it's scared of you.

DEFENDANT:

You talking soft.

LAWYER:

No — I'm talking past your armor, boss.

————

JUDGE:

I've heard the ego speak.

I've heard the logic press.

Now hear the voice that survived the test.

I am the one who felt bullets rewrite his skin,

felt the floor become a ceiling, then learned to begin again —

in a body that didn't answer the same,

in a world that still called my name.

I learned toughness in hospitals and silent nights,

relearning my body, redefining my fight.

Not how to strike back, not how to be feared,

but how to sit with pain and still stay clear.

I met every version of me in that chair:

the angry me, the scared me, the child in despair,

the pride that protected, the ego that lied,

the soul that kept whispering, "You still alive."

Real toughness was not killing a side of me —

it was learning the balance inside of me.

Letting fear speak without letting it drive.

Letting pride exist without letting it decide.

I learned how to respond instead of react,

how to pause when the past tried to pull me back.

How to like without losing control.

How to dislike without losing my soul.

I learned that strength ain't volume or threat —

it's choice.

It's awareness.

It's breath in the chest.

I rose not by hardening, but by becoming whole,

by choosing who I am, not who pain enrolled.

By knowing when to stand, when to walk, when to leave,

when to speak with restraint, when to simply breathe.

So here is the verdict, written in my spine:

The old toughness was survival.

This toughness is design.

The sentence:

Live ruled by reaction and you'll always be chained

to yesterday's trauma, to yesterday's name.

You'll be respected, feared, but never be free,

guarding a version you outgrew to be.

The door:

You can choose now.

Not out of fear — out of awareness.

You can choose your response instead of your reflex.

You can choose balance when ego and anger collide.

You can choose who you become when life applies pressure.

You are not your trigger.

You are not your past.

You are the one who decides

what version of you that would last

That...

is real toughness.

Not hardness.

Not violence.

Not pride.

But the strength to change,

to integrate every part of you,

and to consciously become

who you decide to be.

Court adjourned.

Inner Me — Are You My Enemy?

ME:

The inner me is inner peace.

Look at the love I give to the enemy.

Well… who is he?

It's everyone I see?

Inner peace, just me being free.

Inner me, what you see?

INNER ME:

I see hate, fake hoe ass snakes.

ME:

Inner me, who are they?

Wait… who are you

if they resemble me?

INNER ME:

I'm you — your inner peace.

Everyone else a leech,

trying to get a piece.

ME:

Then why, when I'm alone,

enemy voice still offensive

to me?

Put me on, inner me,

to perspective.

Maybe that

will be my release.

INNER ME:

They try to hold and not let go.

They cowards —

they move better when they see you on the floor.

ME:

How do I detach?

How do I break free?

We gotta come up with a strategy.

INNER ME:

We got it —

it's you and me.

We go get them.

ME:

Who?

INNER ME:

All of them.

Let's do it.

ME:

Gotta defend the inner.

INNER ME:

Look at him.

ME:

Who?

INNER ME:

Son walking across the street.

ME:

What he do?

INNER ME:

I hate niggas!

ME:

Chill…

his appearance offends you?

Altercation 2

ME:

She fake cute.

INNER ME:

Nah, fuck that bitch.

ME:

What? She bad.

INNER ME:

She prolly money hungry with mad kids.

ME:

Damn... here you go again.

Altercation 3

ME:

Bout to step out — I'm flexing.

INNER ME:

You know how we be.

ME:

Boi whip dope.

INNER ME:

Fuck that nigga, cheap ass spokes.

ME:

Huh?

Altercation 4

ME:

We gotta pull up to the store.

INNER ME:

Fuck these hoe niggas — grab the pole.

ME:

What happened?

We beefed with them before?

INNER ME:

Hell nah,

but I'm ready to let it go.

ME:

Temper, temper —

chill, inner me,

before we make another enemy.

Altercation 5

ME:

Hanging with shorty,

she fine as fuck.

Relax — don't fuck it up.

INNER ME:

She got something going.

These hoes be setting shit up.

ME:

Damn…

inner negative as fuck.

INNER ME:

Nah, I got your back up.

You'll be slipping up.

Altercation 6

ME:

Inner me, inner me —

we gotta chop it up.

INNER ME:

What up, my boy?

What the fuck you want?

ME:

I noticed every issue —

you make a problem.

INNER ME:

And you know I'm gonna solve them.

ME:

Shit be peaceful —

you act and bring chaos.

I came to the conclusion.

INNER ME:

Huh?

ME:

People be friends to me.

INNER ME:

Here goes the delusion.

ME:

These hoes be choosing,

and you negative, causing confusion.

INNER ME:

Bro, you live in a fake world —

big illusions.

ME:

Yo, inner me,

I know you protect me,

but you bring chaos.

I know we've been through shit —

now you guarding my freedom.

ME:

All this time, I've been hunting my enemy.

And now I see you.

ENEMY:

Speak —

what you trying to say to me?

ME:

Don't let this shit fuck up your pride.

This shit hurts me.

It actually makes me wanna cry.

Because I realize —

inner me… are you my enemy the whole damn time?

PHASE 4 — UNDERSTANDING

Color: Gold / White Light

State: Clarity

Consciousness: Integration

Structure: 3 Frequencies (I, II, III)

FREQUENCY I — I

The Return to Self

(Reunion, forgiveness, identity no longer split)

This is the moment the inner war ends.

Not by victory, but by recognition.

The parts that once fought for survival

now stand in the same body without armor.

The past is seen.

The wounds are named.

The self is no longer divided against itself.

This is where compassion replaces judgment

and memory is held without bleeding.

We Are

We are not our pain,

we are not our past,

we are the breath that stayed

when the storm hit fast.

We are the rise that followed

every hard collapse,

the proof that the soul can bend

and still not crack.

We are not our scars,

we are not our fear,

we are the quiet voice that said

"keep going" when hope wasn't near.

We are the light in the chest

when the night felt long,

the hum in the dark that whispered

"you still belong."

We are not the chains,

we are not the fall,

we are the strength that learned to crawl

before it learned to stand tall.

We are the rhythm of healing

in a world that rush,

the heartbeat that kept time

when the mind lost trust.

We are the ones who kept breathing

when the air felt thin,

who found God in the silence

and peace within.

We are the ones who turned wounds

into wisdom and flame,

who let the fire teach

instead of leaving a stain.

We buried the shame,

we uncovered the truth,

turned broken into becoming,

old into new.

We are not finished,

we are unfolding still,

writing new chapters

with disciplined will.

When we rise, we rise together,

like tides that pull the moon,

every healed thought

makes the dark retreat sooner.

Every step forward

loosens a hidden chain,

not just in me—

but in the ones who carry the same pain.

So when the world ask,

"Who are you now?"

we answer from spirit,

not ego, not doubt:

We are not what we lost.

We are not what we feared.

We are what remained

when the storm disappeared.

We are the process,

the proof, the flame,

the ones who survived

and didn't stay the same.

We are becoming.

We are free.

We are the healed version

of who we used to be.

Love the Teacher / Fear the Student

I enrolled in love without reading the course,

showed up too early, heart racing, off course.

Happy or sad, disappointed or glad,

smiles on the surface, my spirit was mad.

Emotionally lost, I rushed every test,

trying to pass feelings that never digest.

The syllabus said trust, I skipped that page,

fear was the teacher, doubt in a cage.

Pop-quiz on touch, I froze in my seat,

tenderness shook me, made my pulse retreat.

I wanted to hold you, rewind the time,

but weakness felt foreign, like crossing a line.

So I turned your heart into problems to solve,

treated your love like a case to dissolve.

Thought every soft moment was hiding a trick,

like kindness was poison wrapped up in a gift.

I made suspicion the homework, control the routine,

grading your patience with trauma-stained schemes.

Finals came fast, I wasn't prepared,

you passed your healing, I stayed impaired.

You moved to the next class, new air, new view,

I stayed in the echo of me and you.

Now you fell back—no, you moved on,

I fell behind when the bell rang gone.

Missing your love, your warmth, your tone,

realizing too late what felt like home.

And I say "I knew it, this how it goes,"

but truth is I trained my fear to close.

I was the course, love was the teacher,

fear was the voice, the loud false preacher.

Fear took the quiz, fear chose the route,

fear raised its hand when my soul stayed mute.

I forgot myself in the middle of you,

so I failed my truth and I lost you too.

I was the course, I skipped my own section,

let fear write answers, not self-direction.

Didn't choose me, so I couldn't choose us,

now I'm left with echoes where love once was.

First, I apologize to the man in the mirror—

for letting fear speak louder than spirit,

for handing my heart to doubt as a leader,

for not choosing me when love tried to meet her.

And to you…

I'm sorry for the silence, the distance, the strain,

for turning your softness into my pain.

I was the course. Love tried to teach me.

Fear spoke first… and I let it beat me.

My apologies.

Forgiveness

What is forgiveness?

What does it sound like in silence?

Is it peace in the chest

or a storm learning balance?

Do I pardon intention

when the damage was real?

Do I soften the truth

or accept how I feel?

Do I tell myself "maybe they didn't mean it,"

or do I stand in the fact they did what they did?

Can I love who they are

without loving what happened,

or does healing demand

I stop lying to my ribs?

Forgiveness feel like vision

with the eyelids shut tight,

logic say "hold the grudge,"

but the soul say "release tonight."

The mind keep receipts,

the heart keep the scars,

but the spirit keep whispering,

"Freedom is where you are."

Forgive me…

for looping the same old pain,

for letting yesterday's storms

keep watering today's rain.

For revisiting lessons

I already passed,

for letting disrespect

keep pulling me back.

How you forgive

when the wound still ache?

When the apology never came,

but the memory stayed?

Is it wishing them peace

even when they stole yours?

Is it loving from distance,

not opening doors?

Some days I'm strong.

Some days I'm torn.

Some days I heal.

Some days I mourn.

But I learned the hardest pardon

ain't the ones who crossed me—

it's the man in the mirror

when he lost me.

'Cause the image I hold

and the choices I made

don't always line up

in the light of today.

So guilt sat heavy,

shame made a home,

regret wrote letters

I kept in my bones.

But today I choose flight

over chains in my chest.

I choose breath over blame,

I choose peace over rest.

I choose growth over grief,

truth over fear,

I choose the version of me

that still believes I'm here.

Mistakes ain't my name

unless I answer the call.

They teachers in disguise,

not life sentences at all.

They maps, not prisons,

signs, not walls,

showing where I tripped

so I don't fall.

So every sunrise I renew my vow:

to forgive what was,

to love what's now,

to stay disciplined,

to stay aligned,

to guard my spirit,

to free my mind.

'Cause forgiveness ain't for them—

it's the key to my cage.

It's the door out the past,

it's the ink on my page.

I refuse to live bound

to a chapter that closed,

I honor the lesson,

then I let it go.

I forgive me.

For the nights I stayed small.

I forgive me.

For believing the fall.

I forgive me.

For the time I lost sight.

Now I rise.

Now I breathe.

Now I live in my light.

I'll Give Thanks to Me

I'll give thanks to me—

for every night I survived,

every door I walked through

that sharpened my sight.

Every loss that taught me,

every fall that shaped me,

every storm that tried to break me

but instead rearranged me.

Those experiences weren't curses,

they were classrooms in disguise,

every scar was a lecture,

every tear was a sign.

Not punishment—preparation,

not failure—alignment,

life wasn't trying to end me,

it was building my assignment.

I honor my strength to endure the weight,

to carry pressure and still elevate.

I honor the rise after every collapse,

the will that kept breathing

when the future went black.

Self-love was forged in the quiet alone,

ambition grew roots

where the comfort was gone.

Ideas caught fire,

vision learned form,

discipline took the dream

and gave it a storm.

Even in the body,

I saw the same law—

what you stress, you strengthen,

what you train, you evolve.

Day one was light,

but the vision was heavy,

and consistency turned

"someday" into "ready."

So no matter what eyes remember,

or names they forget,

my spirit leave fingerprints

they can't erase yet.

Energy louder than history,

presence deeper than fame,

even if faces get blurry,

they'll still feel my flame.

Through pain came power.

Through loss came sight.

Through breaking came balance,

through darkness came light.

A new version stood up

from the pieces I bled—

still me,

still rising,

still ahead.

And for that—

not pride, not ego, not flex, not pretend—

just gratitude to the man

who refused to descend.

For the breath I protected,

for the growth I let be,

for the life I kept choosing…

I give thanks to me.

Versions Of Me

(*Final Appearance*)

I thought I was just

Alone in the dark

But truth was

I'd drifted too far from my spark

The journey was pain

I didn't need to go through

But it made me

Remade me

So I found you

————

And here you are

The me I knew

The me who smiled

Just walking into a room

The me who loved

No guard No score

Before the pain

Came knocking at the door

I walked through fire

Through loss through lies

Through prison gates

And tear filled nights

I dropped the mask

I burned the disguise

And now I see me

Through my own eyes

I find you

I hold you

And I swear

This time

I'm never letting go

FREQUENCY II — II

Release of the Old Weight

(Gratitude, closure, letting go without resentment)

This is where the hands finally open.

Not in weakness, but in trust.

The weight of yesterday is acknowledged,

then set down without hatred.

What shaped me is honored.

What limited me is released.

This is where appreciation replaces resistance,

and the heart learns to carry light

without carrying chains.

The Eagle

(*Final Appearance*)

She had to fly

She couldn't stay

Now I'm grateful

because now

I can finally see me

———

I know my way

My perspective changed

I control my thoughts

I choose which ones to entertain

Hey Eagle Eagle

Hey Eagle Eagle

the real me is back again

Before she left

she revealed the real Shakiyl

So thank you Eagle

for giving me time to heal

For helping me see myself

and the strength I concealed

I know where I want to go

I know who I want to be

Thank you Eagle

for guiding me

Love Is Freedom / Care Is Pain

I move in love like a tide with no warning,

you feel me before I speak, like the hush before morning.

No costume on my spirit, no shade on my flame,

love drip from my pores, you can see it in my name.

I love the ponds when they whisper,

the oceans when they roar,

the rain when it cleans what was heavy before.

Ants in the cracks, birds carving sky,

trees teaching patience the way they reach high.

I love the grass for surviving the blade,

the wind for reminding us nothing stays.

Cats in the quiet, dogs loyal and loud,

lions with courage, bears strong and proud.

I love all that breathes, all that grows,

even what never stops to let me know.

I love all people — the loud and the still,

the ones climbing slowly, the ones standing on hills.

The rich with their hunger, the poor with their pride,

the broken, the whole, the ones learning to rise.

Love don't ask questions, don't measure or weigh,

it just shows up and chooses to stay.

But care…

care is a deeper location.

Care is where memory build its foundation.

Care is where echo and heartbeat remain,

where touch got a history, and history got pain.

I loved every woman that stepped in my space,

but when they got close to the guarded place,

my chest would tighten, my spirit would shift —

not from their presence, but from what it predicts.

I'd say, "Come here," with honesty true,

but my past would whisper, "You know what this do."

Too close mean real.

Too real mean risk.

Too much to lose when you once got dismissed.

Because love is freedom —

wide like the sea,

no locks on the heart, just possibility.

But care is where attachment learns your name,

and attachment remembers the language of pain.

So I learned how to love without running in fear,

and guard my heart without pushing love away from here.

Not from coldness.

Not from pride.

But from healing the place where the old me almost died.

Love is freedom.

Care is vulnerability.

And I'm learning to hold both

without letting fear write the story of me.

GOODBYE YESTERDAY

Goodbye yesterday,

I remember you clearly.

I appreciate the experience

even when humiliation

decorated my confidence yearly.

Pain was my professor,

pressure made me apply it.

Yesterday taught the lesson—

today I finally got it.

So I say goodbye yesterday,

not emotional, just precise.

I don't hate where I came from,

I just won't pay that price.

Goodbye to everyone I knew by name.

Goodbye to behaviors

that kept me trapped in the same.

Goodbye to the war I was living inside,

where survival felt normal

and peace felt like a lie.

Goodbye to shame.

Goodbye to the heart rate racing,

body on alert

even when nothing was chasing.

Goodbye to the kind of pain

that trained me to endure,

but never showed me a future—

only taught me how to be sure.

Goodbye yesterday,

my tomorrow won't resemble you.

I outgrew the struggle,

now my vision got a clearer view.

This my last time visiting

who I used to be—

habits, reactions,

patterns that no longer fit me.

Part of me wanna hold on—

that's memory talking loud.

But growth whispered "release,"

and I listened this time around.

So I release you.

Not in anger.

Not in fear.

But with clarity

that places my next step here.

This my final goodbye—

no replay, no return.

Yesterday was the lesson.

Today, I live what I learned.

Goodbye yesterday.

FREQUENCY III — III

Aligned Motion

(Love, presence, moving without fear)

This is where understanding becomes lifestyle.

Not thought.

Not philosophy.

But movement.

The body, the mind, the spirit, and the soul

no longer pull in different directions.

Love is no longer confused with attachment.

Strength is no longer confused with defense.

This is where peace is not imagined —

it is practiced.

My Children

I wish I could walk every path you face,

carry each weight, stand in its place,

hold every moment that tries to bend you,

be the calm when the world pretends you.

At first I showed love the only way I knew—

providing, guiding, seeing you through,

hugs and words, but I never knew

a father's job is to build you too.

Not just to give, but to shape your sight,

to train your heart how to choose what's right,

to show your spirit how to stand in light

when shadows visit the edge of night.

I prayed you wouldn't sink in the deep,

wouldn't lose peace when the pressure speaks,

hoped my storms could water your roots,

turn my lessons into fruit for you to eat.

All the nights when my sky was torn,

I asked God let your days be warm,

let every tear your father cried

become your laughter all through your life.

Paralysis taught me the worth of breath,

the meaning of now, the value of depth,

now I don't ask for easy steps,

I ask for wisdom with every step.

I pray you move through seasons with grace,

smile through change, keep your pace,

never forget your worth, your place,

never trade your truth for a safer space.

Thank you for life, for giving me will,

when hope went quiet, you spoke it still,

you made me stand when my body was still,

made me believe when my heart felt still.

Each of you carry my strength inside,

that steady courage, that quiet pride,

that rooted soul that will not slide—

that's why I know you will rise, not hide.

So hear your father when I speak this truth:

when you start winning, when you step into you,

don't let your past write the rest of you,

don't let old fears define what you do.

I'll lay the path with truth and care,

so you'll know which roads are light, which heavy air,

which bridges hold, which need repair,

so you can move with vision, not with fear.

I love you deeper than words can show,

I'll live the proof of the way you'll grow,

and no matter where your journeys go—

you are already enough.

I love you deeper than words can show,

I'll live the proof of the way you'll grow,

and no matter where your journeys go—

you are already enough.

That's what I know.

Tavion. Shay'aan. Shay'mirr. Leo. Taylor.

I love you.

My Purpose

Tavion —

pure moments, solid motion, love that's grounded,

time we shared was real, every second counted.

Conversations steady, built on truth and calm,

presence like a pillar, you the proof I stand on.

Shay'aan —

one day at a time, you taught my mind to reset,

hope in every smile, every rep, every sweat.

Late nights, early runs, court echoes in the dark,

teaching you to fight, teaching you to breathe, teaching heart.

My son, my pride, my strength in human form,

you the reason I believe when the future calling warm.

Shay'mirr —

Mr. Too Smooth, calm walk, king talk,

confidence quiet, but it roar when you walk.

Our talks got depth, your vision stay wide,

you move like you know you were built to rise.

Keep that smile, let your light stay loud,

you don't chase the crown — you already crowned.

Taylor —

my princess, my sunshine, my joy in the room,

your smile give a strong man space to bloom.

You show me how power can soften its tone,

how love can be gentle and still be grown.

Daddy's heart in your hands, and I'm proud of that truth,

you my reminder that strength still got roots.

Leo —

my youngest, my quiet, my soul in the still,

we sit in the silence and say everything real.

No noise, no rush, just presence that's loud,

two spirits aligned in a peace-filled cloud.

You give me courage just being you,

that's why my steps stay firm when I'm walking through.

To all of you —

I move in love now, not fear, not doubt,

I walk what I learned, I don't talk it out.

I heal in my steps so you inherit light,

not my scars, not my storms, but my sight.

You not my past, you my purpose in motion,

the reason my heart stays open and focused.

Wherever you go, know this truth stays true:

I rise in alignment — and I rise for you.

Closing

The war is no longer loud inside him.

Not because it disappeared,

but because it no longer commands.

The questions that once shook his ground

now stand beside him, not over him.

The past no longer argues for control.

It speaks only as memory, not as master.

He is not searching now.

He is not running.

He is standing in what he understands.

The child, the man, the wounds, the wisdom —

not separated, not in conflict,

but held in one body, one breath, one direction.

Nothing is finished.

But nothing is lost.

This is what it looks like

when a soul stops fighting itself

and starts walking with itself.

You Are Residue Of Yesterday's Thoughts

(Final Appearance)

So I stopped blaming life.

Stopped cursing my fate.

Started changing my thoughts

to change how I wake.

Now I know why I'm solo sometimes —

this wasn't loss, it was prep.

Self-reliance was the lesson

before connection earned and respected.

I had to sit with me raw.

No role. No applause.

Learn to love my own presence

without flexing my scars.

I had to meet me

before anybody could.

I had to meet me —

now I finally would.

So if you staring in glass

and don't like that view,

don't break the mirror —

let the mirror build you.

You not broken.

You delayed.

You not weak.

You remade.

You don't find yourself later.

You build yourself daily.

And one day you realize —

you've been home the whole time.

Soul vs Spirit

(Final Appearance)

Soul — The Final Whisper (Reunion)

I never had to fight to be seen,

I was the light you tucked behind the screen.

Every shadow that tried to dull my flame,

only burned out —

I stayed the same.

I whispered your name when the noise got loud,

stood in your silence when your head hung down.

You drifted away, but I never left,

I was the pulse still beating in your chest.

I ain't new —

I've been your spark from the start,

the quiet drum that's tied to your heart.

The clouds moved back, now I stand in your view,

not a stranger…

but the voice that's you.

———

Narrator — Final Verse (The Reunion)

I see you now…

not the lie that spoke loud,

but the love that waited quiet in the crowd.

The one I left but never left me,

the one that prayed while I couldn't see.

Spirit talked slick,

fed me gold, dressed in blame,

but it was you who held my flame.

I chased that voice through empty years,

you whispered hope through all my fears.

You never gave up,

not once, not ever.

You built a home out of whispers,

and kept the light on forever.

I thought I was forgotten—

but you never lost faith.

I ran to the world,

but you waited at the gate.

Now I'm here.

Now I know.

The truth ain't new—

it's where I was meant to go.

The spirit was my distraction…

but my soul…

my soul is my direction.

What I Overcame

I walked through every altercation.

Sometimes I fail.

Sometimes I turned around.

But for some reason, I always turned back.

Even when I had to hold my breath to do it.

Even when I fell and didn't want to be seen.

Didn't want to be hurt.

I didn't want to hear the noise anymore.

I was tired of the screams — inside and out.

But I got up.

I kept moving through every upset.

Through everyone who gave up on me.

Through the moments when I gave up on myself.

I got up and kept moving.

Belief started as survival.

Then it became acknowledgment.

Acknowledgment became self-awareness.

And when discipline stopped being something I forced

and became something I lived,

confidence stopped being a mask

and became part of my character.

My smile stopped being something I performed.

Love stopped being something I chased.

The weight in my mind began to lift.

Pain stopped holding me so tight.

Loneliness stopped feeling like punishment

and started feeling like a lesson.

Sitting still became awareness.

And awareness changed my perception.

I decided to see myself

not for what hurt me,

but for what I survived.

My vision got clearer than it had ever been.

I wasn't running anymore.

I wasn't hiding.

I wasn't proving.

That's when I realized

I wasn't just getting up anymore —

I was moving forward.

My words became calm.

My presence became steady.

People didn't feel my chaos —

they felt my peace.

And that peace brought connection,

opportunity,

alignment.

Not because I chased it.

Because I became one.

I saw myself.

And for the first time,

I wasn't trying to escape who I was.

My vision became the most important thing to me.

My children are my heart.

My purpose is my direction.

But the foundation is this:

I chose me.

PHASE 5 — FREEDOM

Color: White / Gold Light

State: Sovereignty

Consciousness: Peace, Presence, Wholeness

Structure: 1 Unified Frequency

The storm is no longer inside.

The mind is quiet.

The body is at ease.

The soul is home.

Not searching.

Not proving.

Not healing.

Being.

FREQUENCY I — I

Freedom

(Release, internal peace, joy without attachment, calm breath, self-sovereignty)

No tension in the chest.

No argument in the thoughts.

No shadow chasing light.

Just stillness that knows itself.

This is not escape.

This is my arrival.

Freedom is when nothing inside is at war.

What Is Happiness?

What is happiness?

Is it a place I arrive, or a state I reside?

Is it a city in peace, or a war I survive?

Is it a moment in time, or a way that I move?

Is it a dream in my sleep, or the proof when I choose?

Is it friends and their laughter, the trips and the cheers?

Is it moving with class, with integrity clear?

Is it hope in the dark, is it belief in the light?

Is it standing in truth when you lose the fight?

What is happiness—

Is it bottles and smoke,

Is it loud in the club or the calm in your throat?

Is it silence with self, or the crowd full of noise?

Is it healing alone, or around all your joys?

Is it quiet tears falling, or joy in your peers?

Is it isolation, or presence right here?

Is it running from pain, or facing your fears?

Is it time in the storm, or the peace when it clears?

What is happiness…

and how do I get there?

Happiness is a mindset.

Happiness is discipline.

Happiness is consistency, not coincidence.

It's how you manage emotion when pressure get vicious,

How you respond to the chaos instead of reacting suspiciously.

Happiness is lessons when life get aggressive,

Seeing every altercation as growth, not a sentence.

It's being fine with the loss, with the change, with the go,

Being happy to move on, being happy to grow.

Happy to love with no chains, even when love don't stay,

Happy to release what no longer aligns with your way.

Happiness is acceptance, removing the ego,

Letting pride fall back so your soul can be legal.

Happiness is you.

It's not somewhere you run.

It's a frequency lived when your truth is begun.

It's the courage to be who you see in your sight,

To wake up and walk as your future in light.

So what is happiness?

Authenticity.

Becoming, daily, the vision you hold of you vividly.

Not who they named you.

Not who they shaped you.

But who your spirit been calling

Since before the world tried to break you.

Happiness is not a destination on maps.

It's a residence built in how you react.

And once you move in,

And stop visiting peace,

Happiness stops being a feeling…

…and becomes the frequency you choose to live in

Inspiration

If you drowned yesterday, what does today mean?

How are you searching for tomorrow when you are still wet in your dreams?

Determination in the chest, confidence in the scheme,

But preparation feels absent when you have never been on this scene.

"How could I be ready? I've never stood here before."

But you said that in storms that tried to bury your core.

You survived what you swore you could not survive,

So why does this moment feel different, like it's harder to climb?

"This ain't the same, I never witnessed this pain."

But every level feels new when your level changes.

Remove doubt, remove fear, you too far to retreat,

You didn't walk through the fire just to turn from the heat.

"My fight is gone, I feel weak in my frame."

That's what growth feels like when it shedding your skin.

They got doubt, they got disbelief, they question your flame,

But you still believe in the strength you can't physically see.

And that's why you always achieve,

'Cause belief itself is a trick in the weave.

Be-LIE-f… hear the lie in the word,

Fear sitting silent, trying to poison your nerves.

If confidence missing, presence can't stay,

If you can't see tomorrow, your today start to fade.

So control what you know, and know what you choose,

Let vision lead, not insecurity's view.

Don't move by what shakes you,

Move by what you see.

Not what your fear is projecting—

But who your soul already agreed to be.

The Island Within

The island within…

what a gentle release.

This version of me

moves with a quieter breeze,

frequency softened,

but heavy with peace,

love finally resting

where striving used to be.

The island within…

a place I could reach.

I sit in the quiet,

I play in the noise,

I listen to echoes,

I honor each voice,

but the one I protect now

is the sound of my own.

Acceptance begins

when the soul feels at home.

The island within…

the sun learns my face,

birds translate the wind,

bugs hum in their place.

Every small life

keeps time with the whole,

and the loudest truth

is the calm in my soul.

The silence sings

what the chaos could not—

that peace doesn't shout,

it simply stays.

The island within…

I finally arrived.

Met the version of me

that was always alive.

Not the one shaped by fear,

not the one built to defend,

but the one that keeps growing

without needing to pretend.

I continue to climb,

not to escape, but to see.

I continue to learn

how to rest in being me.

Life taught in storms,

but returned in the calm—

every lesson a wave

that carried me home.

The island within…

no masks, no performing.

Love moves freely here,

no gripping, no warning.

I give it in light,

I receive what aligns,

and let what is not

drift back to its time.

This is not a place.

This is a state.

This is not an ending.

This is a frequency I became.

Author's Message

If you are still here,

if you've read this far,

first let me say thank you for your time.

You may see yourself somewhere in these pages—

maybe in the drowning,

maybe in the questioning,

maybe in the awakening.

And if understanding is where you are now,

then freedom is where you are arriving.

This book will not tell you what to do.

It won't give you a list of rules or steps to follow.

This book is a mirror.

And if you have the courage to look into it,

you may not only see who you are—

you may also see who you want to become,

and find the strength within yourself

to move toward that vision.

So thank you again for walking this with me.

This isn't an easy journey.

But it is a real one.

This was mine.

And you have yours.

And in time,

we will find our smile again—

and continue to smile.

Peace.

Love.

Respect.

Acknowledgments

First, I want to thank my mom for showing me both my flaws and my greatness, for being the first person to truly believe in me. You were my foundation, my first example of strength, and my first experience of unconditional love. I might not have become the man you thought I would be, but I became the man you wanted me to be.

Shout out to my aunts — Aunt Terry, Aunt Tammy, Aunt Hennessy, Aunt Kat, and Aunt Ching — for being there when I needed it the most: for patience, for love, for listening, and for always giving the best advice.

To my sisters — all five of you — and especially my baby sister Latifah, thank you for your smile, for always reaching out, for flying across the country just to see me. And to her husband as well — gratitude extends to you too.

To my cousin Felicia — thank you for being my friend before my accident, and thank you for staying consistent after. You believed in me even when I wasn't myself, and you made sure I didn't forget who I was.

To TA — my best friend, my cousin, and more like my brother than anything else. The only person who ever knew me authentically, who understood my reactions, my silence, my anger, and my heart without me having to explain. You pushed me to reach for more just by your example. When my mom passed and you told me that even though my mom was gone, I could share yours, that meant everything to me. I love you, for sure. Always my brother, always my cousin, always my friend.

Special thanks to DUV — an old friend who helped me see myself.

To my children — the purest shoutout of all. Thank you for always smiling when I come around. Thank you for the love and warmth no one else could fulfill. Taylor, thank you for being my best friend, my sunshine, and the love that keeps me moving forward every day. To my four sons — thank you for giving me hope, for making me want to be the best dad I can be, even in times when I didn't know how. You kept me inspired when I wanted to give up. You made me walk down different roads and map out new paths. I never knew love until you came. I love each of you differently, but all the same. Through pain, you gave me a reason to smile. Through setbacks, you gave me a reason to rise. You are the foundation of my purpose. Thank you for believing in me. Thank you for seeing me as Superman even when I felt like just a man.

To every woman who crossed my path, every person who played a role in my life, every soul who added a lesson, a mirror, or a moment — I thank you.

And now, I acknowledge myself — the version of me who refused to quit, who kept getting up, who kept believing, who kept choosing growth over bitterness, vision over limitation, and purpose over pain.

Finally, I thank life itself — every adversity, every obstacle, every closed door, every failure, every fall. Everything was either a lesson or a blessing guiding me toward my destination. Every experience shaped my vision, strengthened my discipline, and aligned me with who I was meant to become.

About the Author

My name is Shakiyl Muhammad.

I'm from Rochester, New York.

I had to fall many times just to understand who I am today.

I had to learn what it meant to lose in order to finally understand what winning really is.

This book is a journey through experiences I was submerged in, but it is also about the outcome—what I overcame, what I understood, and what I became. Success, to me, is not a title or a number. It's a state of being. It's how you see yourself. It's how you feel when you're alone with your own reflection.

Real success began the day I learned how to smile without an audience.

The day I became genuinely at peace with who I am.

The day I realized happiness didn't need permission.

That inner peace, that self-acceptance, that quiet joy—

that is The Island Within.

But you don't arrive there without traveling through the storms.

You don't reach the Island Within without first moving through

The Healing Process.

www.ingramcontent.com/pod-product-compliance
Lightning Source LLC
Chambersburg PA
CBHW041311120726
48005CB00014B/1954